SHORT

SW...

PAUL HANNON

HILLSIDE PUBLICATIONS
20 Wheathead Crescent
Keighley
West Yorkshire
BD22 6LX

First Published 2010

© Paul Hannon 2010

ISBN 978 1 907626 04 3

*The sketch maps are based on 1947 OS one-inch maps
and earlier OS six-inch maps*

Cover illustration: The Swale at Ramps Holme, Muker
Back cover: Calver Hill from Maiden Castle
Page 1: Ivelet Bridge
(Paul Hannon/Hillslides Picture Library)

Printed by Steffprint
Unit 5, Keighley Industrial Park
Royd Ings Avenue
Keighley
West Yorkshire
BD21 4DZ

CONTENTS

INTRODUCTION

The valley of the Swale is very well defined, from its beginnings in the tumbling becks of the wild Pennines to its departure from the National Park near Richmond. The remoteness of this northernmost of the Yorkshire Dales has helped it remain relatively quiet and unchanged: with no disrespect to all the other beautiful valleys, it must be said that Swaledale is a bit special. From Keld to Richmond the dale loses little grandeur, remaining steep-sided all the way to that splendidly characterful gateway town. Principal side valley is Arkengarthdale, which shares the characteristics of the main dale: the Arkle Beck is a fast-flowing tributary rising on the moors near Tan Hill. In Swaledale you walk in good company, for the Pennine Way crosses the valley head and the Coast to Coast Walk runs the length of the dale.

Outside of Richmond the dale's attractions are largely of the natural variety, from rolling heather moors to the effervescent river, with waterfalls and deep side valleys in abundance. Reeth is at the heart of things, while Gunnerside and Muker rank superlatives among a chain of delectable villages. There are two distinct types of walking in Swaledale, from flower-filled meadows to mining-ravaged hillsides, two aspects that are its very trademark. No other dale boasts such a wealth of riverbank paths, and no other has such a concentration of remains of the lead mining industry. Evidence abounds, from the mines on the moors down through the gills with their smelt mills to the villages with their miners' cottages. Many of the paths you follow lead to old workings slowly blending back into the hillsides. There is an impressiveness and a beauty about these places which stem partly from an image of hardy 19th century souls who would walk miles daily to toil in dark, damp holes.

Most walks are on rights of way with no access restrictions. Several also make use of 'Right to Roam' to cross Open Country: these areas can be closed for up to 28 days each year subject to advance notice, though only Walk 12 is likely to be affected by grouse shooting. Most walks can be accessed by bus: a service links Richmond and Reeth, then less frequently to Keld. Whilst the route description should be sufficient to guide you around each walk, a map is recommended for greater information: Ordnance Survey 1:25,000 scale maps give the finest detail, and Explorer OL30 covers all but one walk (Explorer 304 covers the other).

USEFUL INFORMATION

·Yorkshire Dales National Park (01756-751600)
·Reeth National Park Centre (01748-884059)
·Richmond Tourist Information (01748-828742)
·Yorkshire Dales Society (01729-825600)
·Open Access (0845-100 3298) www.countrysideaccess.gov.uk
·Traveline - public transport information (0870-6082608)

OTHER TITLES IN THIS SERIES

·UPPER WENSLEYDALE   ·LOWER WENSLEYDALE
·UPPER WHARFEDALE   ·LOWER WHARFEDALE
·MALHAMDALE   ·RIBBLESDALE   ·NIDDERDALE
·INGLETON & WESTERN DALES ·SEDBERGH & DENTDALE
·HARROGATE & KNARESBOROUGH   ·RIBBLE VALLEY
·AROUND PENDLE ·AMBLESIDE & LANGDALE ·BORROWDALE
·BOWLAND ·AIRE VALLEY ·ILKLEY & WASHBURN VALLEY

Walking Country guides to more detailed walks include
·SWALEDALE   ·WENSLEYDALE   ·WHARFEDALE
·NIDDERDALE   ·THREE PEAKS   ·MALHAMDALE
·HOWGILL FELLS   ·TEESDALE   ·EDEN VALLEY

Visit www.hillsidepublications.co.uk

SWALEDALE

20 Short Scenic Walks

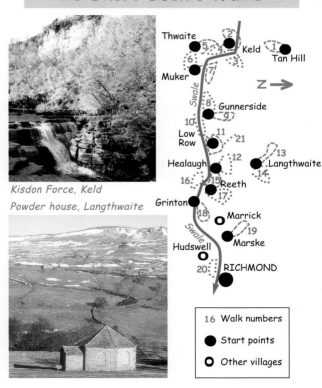

Kisdon Force, Keld

Powder house, Langthwaite

Thwaite
Keld
Tan Hill
Muker
Swale
Gunnerside
Low Row
Healaugh
Langthwaite
Reeth
Grinton
Marrick
Marske
Hudswell
RICHMOND
Swale

16	Walk numbers
●	Start points
○	Other villages

A RECORD OF YOUR WALKS

WALK	DATE	NOTES
1		
2		
3		
4		
5		
6		
7		
8		
9		
10	23/5/12	
11		
12		
13		
14		
15		
16		
17		
18		
19		
20		
21		

3³⁄₄ miles from Tan Hill

Moorland paths amid the bleak surrounds of Britain's highest pub

Start Tan Hill Inn
(GR: 897066), roadside parking
Map OS Explorer OL30, Yorkshire Dales North/Central
or Explorer OL19, Howgill Fells & Upper Eden Valley
Access Open Access, see page 5

At 1725ft/526m the Tan Hill Inn is renowned as the highest pub in the land. The apparently wild moorlands all around are pitted with old coal mines which largely served lead smelting mills in Swaledale and Arkengarthdale. Minor but important roads arrive from Keld via Stonesdale, Reeth via Arkengarthdale, and Stainmore via Barras. Tan Hill was a meeting place of old drovers and packhorse ways, and today catches the large passing trade of tourists, in summer at least: Pennine Wayfarers view the pub as a veritable oasis. Winters are a different matter, the harsh climate and enforced isolation having seen less resilient landlords survive only one before accepting defeat. Each May a long-established sheep show is a major event. The place has also found its way into the news at regular intervals: a double glazing advertisement and ensuing planning problems will be remembered by many; a wrangle over geographical identity featured a temporary transfer to Durham from its rightful county; while Tan Hill is now licensed to perform marriage ceremonies on the premises: Gretna no more!

From the pub cross the road and head away on the broad track of the Pennine Way, this first section being an old mine track. Rising very slightly it affords excellent views: to the right is the skyline of Nine Standards Rigg, while to the left, above you, is the sprawl of Rogan's Seat. At a bend left the Pennine Way bears right, and becomes immediately grassier to run a splendid, largely level course for some time. The slightest of declines leads to crossing the beginnings of a small gill: keep straight on, soon dropping more purposefully as a good grassy path to the right, nearing the road below. In front over the head of Swaledale are the broad shoulders of Great Shunner Fell, with Lovely Seat to its left and to its right the Mallerstang ridge of High Seat.

When the Pennine Way drops into the adjacent ravine to cross the sidestream of Lad Gill, don't follow it but simply continue straight down rougher terrain on a scruffy track to the road below, just above a stone-arched bridge on the gill. Turn right for half a mile's gentle rise along the road. Note that to ensure dry feet you would have to remain on the moorland road back to the start, as an impending section by the beck can be appreciably moist... As the road starts to swing right to climb steeply by another side gill, leave it and drop left on a track through reeds to some crumbling sheepfolds alongside Stonesdale Beck. The track crosses at a ford, but all you need do is turn upstream the few yards to a footbridge just beneath a confluence with Thomas Gill. Again don't cross, but trace a thin and intermittently moist path near the bank of the stream, improving as it runs closer to it. Passing a stone fold on the other bank above a little waterfall, just beyond is a tiny outcrop projecting above a confluence. The path turns right here to rise with Tan Gill, a grand little climb to ultimately gain the road with the pub just five minutes distant.

Tan Hill Inn

4¹₂ miles from Keld

**Beautiful moments on and
around the youthful Swale**

*Start Village centre
(GR: 892011), car park
Map OS Explorer OL30,
Yorkshire Dales North/Central (or Explorer OL19)*

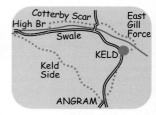

From the square climb to the main road and turn left. A little beyond a walled track on the left take a stile: dropping down a little, cross to a stile ahead. Here begins a fieldpath marked by a string of stiles: in early summer these rich meadows ensure a delectable path. After a second successive barn, slant right up a track to a gate onto the road just left of a house in the hamlet of Angram. Go left to the phone box and take a side road right. Leave immediately by a gate on the right, and a sunken way rises up the field. Just beyond an old limekiln you pass through a gate for a brief enclosed section, then the track heads away, becoming fainter as it slants up rough pasture to a gate in a wall. Extensive views look over Keld to Rogan's Seat, and back over Angram backed by Lovely Seat. Follow a wall away along the edge of a tract of heather moor, and as it drops away contour on to a wall-stile ahead.

Head away on a thin way, crossing a reedy dip to a stile in the facing wall. Now bear gently left up the pasture, with a large tract of heather moor across Ay Gill ahead. A path forms at a ruinous wall corner, and this grassy way runs on above stream and wall. It drops to run along to join the wall, and quickly takes a stile in it onto the heather moor. A clear path runs left to a stile back out at the end: at around 1410ft/430m this is the summit of the walk on Keld Side. Sweeping views to the high watershed of the Swale feature the High Seat ridge and Nine Standards Rigg. Over to the right the limestone of Cotterby Scar is well seen: shortly you shall be walking above that. A thinner but still clear path now runs very gently down through moor grass to a wall-stile. More scattered heather is entered as the path runs on to drop down to a shooters' track, reached by a simple bridge on Blackburn Beck.

The continuing path is indicated by a small cairn opposite: head away on a broad, grassy section between heather. A faint path slants left up this to an early fork: the right turn sees a clearer path form in the heather, down to a ladder-stile off the moor. Two pastures are crossed diagonally to a third such stile. A clear track completes the slant down to a firm track by the river, go right to the road at High Bridge. Turn right, passing a waterfall on the Swale before climbing above the river for a prospect of the confluence with Whitsundale Beck. Dropping back to the river, cross stone-arched Low Bridge at the start of Cotterby Scar. As the track climbs away past a limekiln, leave it on reaching the first trees, by a gateway in the old wall on the right. A thin path heads away to commence a level stroll above the length of the largely unseen cliff.

From a gate at the end the way shadows a wall across open pasture, with Wainwath Force largely obscured by trees below. Keep straight on the field top to a gate onto a road, crossing to the drive to East Stonesdale Farm. Approaching Stonesdale Beck, the unsung gem of Currack Force is just off-route before the bridge. A little pull precedes a level stroll to the farm, where a track turns down through a gate to drop steeply to East Gill Force, a delectable spot. Take the path down the near side of the waterfall to a foot-bridge on the Swale. The path climbs right, and keep right to run enclosed back along to re-enter the square. *East Gill Force*

SWINNER GILL

*3¹₂ miles
from Keld*

**The Swale Gorge hides a
dramatic ravine that this
walk eagerly explores**

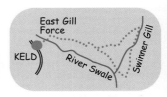

Start **Village centre (GR: 892011), car park**
Map **OS Explorer OL30, Yorkshire Dales North/Central**

Keld is the first outpost of any size in Swaledale. Most buildings huddle around a tiny square below the road and high above the Swale. Park Lodge offers refreshments, while close by are a chapel with a fine old sundial of 1840, and WCs. The fact that this delectable spot marks the junction of Pennine Way and Coast to Coast Walk was insufficient to save its youth hostel from closure: today's Keld Lodge may be a more expensive replacement, but it has brought licensed premises back for the first time since the closure of the Cat Hole Inn in the 1950s.

Leave the bottom right corner of the square by a broad, walled path past a barn. Quickly reaching a fork, take the left branch dropping steeply to a footbridge on the Swale. Across, a path curves up above the beautiful waterfall of East Gill Force to a famous junction where Pennine Way and Coast to Coast Walk part company. Turn right over the stone-arched bridge and a broad track rises away, up through a gate and on above a steep, fenced scree slope high above the gorge. At the end it opens out to swing round past a barn beneath lead mining remains to a fork. You will return by the left branch, so for now take the stony track slanting right down with the old wall. This drops through trees to wind down to a gate at the bottom and on to a bridge on Swinner Gill.

The track slants up a steep little bank behind then runs on into open terrain. You, however, leave within a couple of minutes at the start of a fenced enclosure just up to the left. The faintest of paths rises to the fence corner then doubles back left, slanting up into bracken as it becomes clearer. Remain on this as it later eases to reveal the colourful enclave of Swinner Gill you are about to penetrate. It runs delightfully on into the gill, enjoying waterfalls and gleaming scars. Over a stile in an arrow-like fence above another waterfall you quickly slant in to join the stream itself, above yet another waterfall. Amid rugged surrounds water gushes from an arched level. Cross here to a clear path climbing out the other side. Ignore an early left fork and continue climbing, rising through a modest rocky band to commence a super level walk to meet a broader path just short of a stone-arched bridge on Swinner Gill. Just across the gill at the foot of the side valley of East Grain stand the remains of a lead smelting mill.

Double back left, rising across a small spoilheap and keeping right at an early fork to slant delightfully up across this heather flank. Look back into the gill to see a fine waterfall beneath the smelt mill. The path runs on through a few rocks to a gate in a wall. The grassy way swings right to run through bracken down past an old mine building and beneath more spoil to drop down alongside Crackpot Hall. This former farmhouse was abandoned long ago as a result of mining subsidence: its view down the Swale Gorge remains spectacular. The continuing track soon merges with your outer one to retrace steps to Keld.

East Grain, Swinner Gill

*3³⁄₄ miles
from Keld*

**Even by Upper Swaledale's
high standards this is an
awesome, beautiful walk**

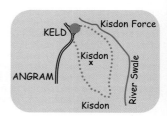

*Start Village centre (GR: 892011), car park
Map OS Explorer OL30, Yorkshire Dales North/Central*

Leave the tiny square by the road rising left to the main road, and turn left on it until a walled track drops left by a barn. This is the first section of an old corpse road which ran all the way down the valley to what was then the only church at Grinton: for the deceased of Keld, it was only the start of a long trip to the burial ground. On crossing a tiny beck by ford and slab footbridge it begins to climb steeply away, soon opening out until it slants up open pasture as a fine green way. Dalehead mountains on view are Lovely Seat, Great Shunner Fell, High Seat and Nine Standards Rigg, while just opposite is the hamlet of Angram.

Easing further the track runs on beneath an isolated house, and when it swings left to serve it an even nicer green way continues to a gate in a wall ahead. A long pasture is crossed, rising gently until approaching Hooker Mill Scar just ahead, it swings left up to a gate in the parallel wall. Rising to another such wall-gate it then runs between long abandoned walls by some mining debris. Through a further gateway it runs delightfully on the edge of moorland: Kisdon's unfrequented summit stands at 1637ft/499m a good half-mile over to the left. Arrival at a wall-gate finally marks the walk's summit at around 1607ft/490m. By now the first views ahead feature moors across the gorge leading round to Rogan's Seat. The way drops away with a wall on the left, revealing Swinner Gill, Arn Gill and the Ivelet scars opposite, and more of the main valley ahead.

As the green track veers away from it, remain on a fainter wallside way a little further to a gate in the wall just past a memorial stone. Taking five minutes on Open Access land, pass through and drop down to an outer wall corner just below, then continue down the steeper wallside, through a few rocks at the bottom onto the Pennine Way overlooking the Swale Gorge. Turn left to commence a classic walk along a near-level terrace passing through assorted gateways and stiles and occasional rashes of stones. It traverses Kisdon's flank in glorious fashion, with spectacular views over the finest section of the Swale backed by Arn Gill and Swinner Gill under Rogan's Seat.

Eventually a wooded bank comes in on the right, and the path follows the hillside round to the left for a sustained spell. In time a fork is reached at a gap in the accompanying wall: pass through to slant down to a junction with a broader path. Keld is just a few minutes to the left, but for a short detour to view Kisdon Force, go right. Just down a slope is a gateway in the wall on the left, and from it a path drops through trees to a viewpoint for the waterfall: the descent to the riverbank is somewhat steep but the scene is a fine one. To return to Keld rejoin the top path and go back along to the right, passing beneath tall cliffs before the way becomes enclosed to re-enter the village square.

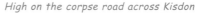

High on the corpse road across Kisdon

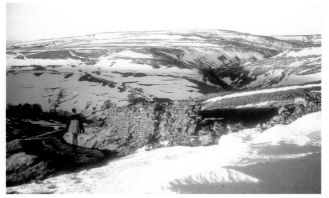

4½ miles from Thwaite

Moorland and meadows on the flanks of an endearing hill

Start Village centre
(GR: 892981), roadside parking
Map OS Explorer OL30,
Yorkshire Dales North/Central

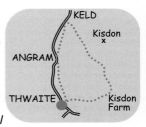

Thwaite is a tiny village that was birthplace of Richard and Cherry Kearton, pioneers in nature photography. The Kearton Country Hotel serves refreshments: turn along the side road in front of it, and at the end a Pennine Way sign points through a ginnel just right of a farmyard: a couple of stiles lead into a field where the path forks. Go left on the Pennine Way, across to a gate and on a grass track to a farm bridge over Skeb Skeugh. Bear right up the steep field, merging with a wall to rise to a corner stile onto open moorland. A super path slants up through heather to a wall corner, with fine views back over the village to Lovely Seat, Buttertubs Pass and Great Shunner Fell. Head on with the wall above a barn with a glimpse of Muker, up to a stile and on with a wall on your left. This curves round to become briefly enclosed, on through a small gate then swings right with the wall to the rear of Kisdon Farm.

Passing through a gate at the end onto the drive, instead take a gate on the left from where a green walled way rises past an old limekiln. Quickly opening out at a fork the Pennine Way turns right: your way is left, on a grassy track climbing by the wallside. Higher it becomes enclosed to emerge into a higher pasture, where the way slants up to meet the opposite wall then rises left with it to a gate. At around 1607ft/490m this is the summit of the walk. The splendid track heads away across open country, with heather rolling away to Kisdon's unfrequented summit a good half-mile to the right. Through a gate the way runs between old walls and past mining debris to a gate, then on to another in the next parallel wall. Ahead are big views to the high fells encircling the dalehead.

The way now swings right across a long pasture, with an isolated house ahead. Pass through a gate at the end just beyond which its access track comes in. Together advance on well below the house, still a splendid track as it slants more steeply down, meeting a wall then becoming fully enclosed for the final section down to a tiny stream crossing, with ford and slab bridge. Just up the other side it meets the valley road. Go briefly left to a stile on the left, then drop down a little and cross to a stile ahead. Here begins a fine fieldpath marked by stiles: in early summer these flower-rich meadows ensure a clear, delectable path. A further guide is a string of isolated field barns that are all passed on their right.

A brow beneath the hamlet of Angram reveals Thwaite with Lovely Seat above: to your left Kisdon's western flank remains a splendid sight throughout. The road is rejoined at a stile after skirting Angram, and within a couple of minutes is vacated again at a gate/stile on the left. Slant down to a stile beyond an island barn, then on to bridge a sidestream. Through a stile behind follow the left-hand wall away through several pastures. At a stile by a barn the wall ends and you cross a domed field to a stile/barn at the end. A moist corner leads on, now alongside tree-lined Skeb Skeugh. An intermittent flagged path runs to a corner stile, then an embanked path bears left to another. Through a gate/stile pass left of barns to a stile back onto the ginnel by which you left the village.

Summer meadows at Angram

3½ miles from Muker

A simple walk offering good views from low slopes, and linking two lovely villages

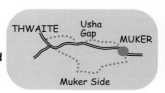

Start Village centre (GR: 910978), car park at east end
Map OS Explorer OL30, Yorkshire Dales North/Central

Muker is a fine centre for the upper dale, with the Farmers Arms and a shop/tearoom. This is probably Swaledale's most picturesque village: prominent in most views is St Mary's church, another notable building being the 1868 Literary Institute. The old school is now a crafts shop and gallery, tablets proclaim that the famous Kearton brothers of Thwaite were former pupils. The village pound stands by the car park entrance. Muker is the venue for the Swaledale Agricultural Show in September. The River Swale rejoins the main road below the village, after their enforced split by Kisdon. Cross the bridge at the east end of the village and leave the road immediately after the car park by a walled track rising right. This is known as the Occupation Road (farmers' access to the various fields), and beyond some barns it doubles back to climb towards Muker Side. Increasingly magnificent views look across the valley to Kisdon, while beyond Muker is the Swale Gorge backed by Rogan's Seat.

Ultimately the way swings left to rise to a T-junction of walled tracks at Three Loaning (lane) End. Go right for a near-level stride along Muker Side, a super section with outstanding views over the upper dale, in particular across to Kisdon, while Great Shunner Fell impresses straight ahead. Just beyond crossing a stone-arched bridge on a tiny stream, turn right down a walled, grassy way as far as a tiny barn on a bend. Here leave by a gate on the left, crossing a field-bottom to become briefly enclosed again before a continuing track passes above renovated Appletree Thwaite. Merging with its drive at a gate at the end, follow it down through a further gate then down a larger field to find a stile just

18

to its right in the bottom corner. This gives a tiny short-cut over a footbridge on Cliff Beck in a little ravine. The track is rejoined just beyond to run out onto the road, with Thwaite just along to the left beyond the Hawes junction. For a note on Thwaite see Walk 5.

Turn along the short lane in front of the Kearton teashop, and at the end a Pennine Way sign points the way through a ginnel by a house just right of a farmyard: a couple of stiles lead into a field. Here the Way strikes left, but you continue with Thwaite Beck to a wall-stile ahead. Here leave it for a thin path across three further fields to reach a stone-arched footbridge on a smaller beck, Skeb Skeugh, coming in from the left. Beyond a stile head away with a wall to a stile at the end, then on past a barn to a stile from where a short, enclosed beckside track joins the road at Usha Gap Bridge. Go briefly left along the road to the farm and up to the house. Go right through the yard to a gate into a camping field, then bear left to find a stile near the far end of the field. A string of obvious stiles now leads a faint path across the field-bottoms to Muker, waiting ahead. The latter stages of the path are flagged: on entering the village, a little snicket on the right drops down to emerge at the pub.

Looking back to Muker and Kisdon from the Occupation Road

*4¹2 miles
from Muker*

**A lofty promenade high
above the riverbank by
which you return**

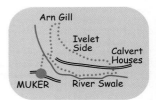

Arn Gill

Ivelet
Side

Calvert
Houses

MUKER   River Swale

Start Village centre (GR: 910978), car park at east end
Map OS Explorer OL30, Yorkshire Dales North/Central
Access Open Access, see page 5

For a note on Muker see page 18. Leave by a road slanting
up behind the Literary Institute at a triangular green. Pass to the
right of an 'island' residence and on past the former Post office to
a gate/stile into a field. Initially a track, by the next gate/stile it
becomes a stone-flagged path crossing seven fields linked by solid
stiles to arrive at the riverbank. Turn right to another stile to follow
the Swale downstream the few yards to Ramps Holme Bridge. This
tall footbridge makes an excellent viewpoint for the lonely Swale
Gorge. Across, rise a few steps to a fork then go left up to a level
path. Follow this left and as it quickly drops down to meet a stony
track, double sharply back right up it. Soon levelling out, make use
of Open Access and take an inviting grassy way slanting back left.

This gives a mercurial climb through Ivelet Wood, raking
ever gently up the flank to break free of colourful scrub. Views
open out over the Swale Gorge and across to Kisdon. Ultimately it
curves round to approach the small sidestream of Arn Gill, reached
via mining spoil: just across is a stone hut. Without crossing take a
slim trod climbing right, shadowing the near side of the gill up to a
stone-arched level beneath a small crag. Here you meet the thin
trod of a public footpath. Double back right on this, rising gently
to open out high above the dale floor. It slowly levels out as the
modest escarpment of Ivelet Boards forms above. Be aware that a
moderately 'hairy' section awaits: if slippery conditions prevail, an
option would be to rise to easier ground above the scar.

Advance on to approach scattered trees and through modest scree, easing out on Ivelet Side above further minor scars. A low wall survives alongside, and as this drops away bear left from the fading edge: an improving way contours off round grass slopes. Passing beneath Kisdon Scar and above an old walled quarry, Calvert Houses is revealed below. The grassy track now drops gently down, passing above a dark, limestone fissure. Just beyond, at a slight dip, bear off right to drop to the road between low scars directly above the hamlet. Turn down its short access road into the yard, and take a stile on the left. Head away with the wall to a corner stile, and from one just behind it slant down the field on the right to a gate in a fence. A track then slants down the next field with the river just below. As it fades drop to a small gate to pick up the valley path. Don't pass through but follow the path down to the right to join the riverbank and head upstream. The path alongside the Swale witnesses some good scenery as it flows over a wide, stony bed.

After a short mile the path cuts out a bend in the river by being deflected by a small wooded bank, on through a gateway where a track drops down, then briefly back with the river as you advance on through a gate/stile back onto the bank. At a stile at the end leave the river to cross several stiles in parallel walls to pass Ramps Holme Farm. From a stile by a barn beyond, a path runs on above a wall to rejoin the outward route, down to cross Ramps Holme Bridge and retrace steps to Muker.

Old lead workings, Arn Gill

3¹2 miles
from Gunnerside

**Archetypal Swaledale
meadows lead to the
valley's finest bridge**

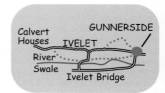

Start Village centre (GR: 951981), parking by bridge
Map OS Explorer OL30, Yorkshire Dales North/Central

For a note on Gunnerside see page 26. From the bridge,
depart along the lane to the right of the main up-dale road: it is
identified by a tidy little green at its start. This soon ends at the
school, and a gate to its right leads between modern housing to a
stile into a field. A little path heads across meadows punctuated by
a string of stiles (and one gate) to arrive at a bend of the Swale at
Marble Scar. Don't take the stile towards the river but go right up
the fence to a stile at the top above a wooded bank. Now resume
as before, through a longer series of stiles to wooded Shore Gill.
Drop down to cross a footbridge and up the other side into Ivelet.
As you enter note a 1761 datestone by the estate office.

Ivelet is a tiny hamlet, off the beaten track and best
known for its bridge, reached by turning down the road to the
river, and just a few minutes upstream. This beautiful old high-
arched structure is unquestionably the finest crossing of the
Swale (illustrated on page 1). Your route, however, takes a gate on
the right to accompany the Swale upstream. An intermittent path
initially follows the river until deflected right to pass through a
small gate at the end of the second field. Instead of returning to
the river slant up to the right, a track forming to rise to a gate in
the fence above. Slant left above it to find a stile in the wall above
near the top left corner. The hamlet of Calvert Houses could be
accessed by another stile just to the left, but you simply ascend
the fieldside to a small gate at the top corner. Now ascend more
steeply left to another small gate by a ruined barn in front of some

cottages. This puts you onto the Calvert Houses access road. A few yards above it joins another minor access road.

Turn right for a delightful traffic-free stroll, enjoying grand views from this shelf under the moor edge high above the valley. Further on it drops down by lush, grassy verges to a junction on a brow behind Gunnerside Lodge, Swaledale's premier shooting lodge. Here drop left, the road crossing a bridge and climbing away past Shoregill Head before levelling out along the foot of open moor. As it starts to drop gently down take a broad shooters' track branching up to the left, between two farms on the right at Dyke Heads. Ahead are sweeping views over the valley, with Gunnerside itself just ahead. As the track curves left around the hillside before reaching Gunnerside Gill, you reach a substantial cairn. This sends a thin path slanting right down initially reedy pasture. Lower down the terrain improves and a lovely grassy continuation approaches a fence enclosing the wooded gill to reveal the roofs of Gunnerside below: now descend a little more steeply right to an unfenced road as it crosses a cattle-grid to enter the village, or follow the fence down to a small gate in the very corner to drop down into the centre opposite the village hall.

The Swale at Marble Scar

*3¹4 miles
from Gunnerside*

**A fascinating exploration of
this deeply confined valley,
with mining remains to
stir the imagination**

Start Village centre (GR: 951981), parking by bridge
Map OS Explorer OL30, Yorkshire Dales North/Central

For a note on Gunnerside see page 26. Leave the bridge by an access track on the pub side, following Gunnerside Beck upstream. After being deflected outside Gunnerside Hall small pastures lead a faint path along more open surrounds until a stile puts you into a wooded bank of the beck. A clearer path now runs by the beck, and a few boulders, on through a small gate and into denser trees. A grand walk leads through this long sliver of lovely woodland from where you rise above the beck. The wood is left in impressive surrounds as you near Gunnerside Beck again, dropping down to a plank bridge out of the trees into an open strath: adjacent stiles send you along a wallside and on through two further wall-stiles to arrive at the site of a crushing mill. A long row of bunkers just up behind was for storing the lead ore.

Just past the ruins along this lawn-like flat pasture you reach a fence-stile. Here a path rises to run along a wallside to emerge above a steep bank dropping to the beck. The substantial ruin opposite is a former mine shop, an office building of the Sir Francis Mine. Here you abandon the valley floor at a stile in the adjacent wall. An inviting, broad green path slants up through bracken, keeping eyes peeled for an early crossroads with a lesser path (before the first wall corner is reached). Turn right on this to slant across to approach a sturdy descending wall. Pass right of a low ruin in front of the wall to find an extremely narrow stile in it. Continue across the tops of two fields (no path), emerging into open pasture to advance on a short embanked section. Pass a tiny section of wall (an old sheep shelter) and on towards a wall beyond. Keep well above it to rise gently onto a delectable green track.

This runs on, becoming part enclosed to reach the house at Winterings: Low Scar rises above. Easiest option follows the drive out and all the way down to Gunnerside, but a nicer field-path awaits. So, enter the garden by the gate/stile in front and pass round to the right of the house (to its front). Cross the paddock in front of it to a stile in the wall ahead, out into a field. Here begins a splendid crossing of numerous fields, linked by stiles in intervening walls. Midway there is even a short section of embanked old path down into a dip. At the end you approach three buildings, the middle one just a barn. Pass right of the left-hand cottage of Pot Ing and on to a gate just beyond, where its grassy drive drops away in sunken fashion. Over a stream and through a gate it rises to meet a now surfaced access road. Turn right on this to spiral steeply down into Gunnerside, far below. This gentle byway affords a classic bird's-eye view over the rooftops.

The mine shop, Gunnerside Gill

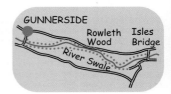

*4³⁄₄ miles
from Gunnerside*

**A simple, intimate
riverside stroll**

*Start Village centre (GR: 951981), parking by bridge
Map OS Explorer OL30, Yorkshire Dales North/Central*

Gunnerside, like most of its neighbours, had its heyday in lead mining times, when it was a busy centre for that thriving industry. It was founded by the Norsemen, and it seems Gunnar was a Viking chieftain. There is the Kings Head pub, a tearoom, WCs and a museum at the old smithy. The Literary Institute of 1877 serves as village hall, and there is a Wesleyan Methodist Chapel of 1806. The village stands astride its own beck, which apart from a level quarter-mile from here to the Swale, spends its time tumbling down the deep gill immediately above the village.

Take the up-dale road out of the village, shadowing Gunnerside Beck to its confluence with the Swale at Gunnerside New Bridge. Across it, leave rapidly, before the Crackpot junction by a wall-stile on the left. Rise to a small gate above, then up onto a hard track just above that. This is Dubbing Garth Lane, which leads unfailingly left down-dale. After a stony drop to river level it settles down to a delectable grassy course, largely between walls other than when the Swale is alongside. Open views look to Rowleth Wood on the north bank and Harkerside Moor down-dale. Towards the end it becomes stonier again to run through trees to Haverdale House Farm. Becoming surfaced it quickly reaches a junction with a through road. Turn left and keep left to soon reach the three arches of Isles Bridge. Attractive cottages occupy the far bank.

Cross the bridge and use a stile on the left to commence the return, immediately abandoning the river to enter undergrowth. Emerging, the path bears left along a field and small stream, but rather than rejoining the returning Swale it turns away, bearing right by a very low wall. Crossing the stream, leave the scrubby bank on the right before aiming across the centre of a large pasture. Wooden boards at the end cross a linear swamp to a stile behind, then bear right with a wall. Just past a chalet take a gap-stile in the wall and join a grass track running left to join the valley road as it approaches the returning Swale.

Follow the road left through the foot of Rowleth Wood, and as it starts to rise away rejoin the river's bank, a path negotiating scrub before quickly opening out to run a lovely part-wooded course tight by the Swale. At a stile at the end it is forced back onto the road at a steep, wooded bank. Head along to another stile, but without setting foot on tarmac take an adjacent gate into a field, and a track drops steeply away. The village can be seen ahead beyond innumerable parallel walls. Bear left to the river, and before the field-end a small gate in the adjacent wall puts you back onto the Swale's bank. A path now follows it pleasurably back to Gunnerside New Bridge. Just before Gunnerside Beck and the bridge, turn for the village at a gate by a barn and cross to a squeezer-stile in the tapering corner. Advance to another into a barnyard, keeping right of the barns to a stile at the end. Through an unkempt corner you emerge into the last field, using a stile at the first buildings to emerge back into the centre, conveniently alongside the pub.

The Swale at Rowleth Wood

4½ miles
from Low Row

Low Row's attractive surrounds feature a super combination of riverside and moorland rambling

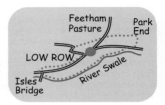

Feetham Pasture
Park End
LOW ROW
River Swale
Isles Bridge

Start Village centre (GR: 987984), roadside parking
Map OS Explorer OL30, Yorkshire Dales North/Central

Low Row straddles the valley road for a good mile, and incorporates the twin hamlet of Feetham. A long open 'green' runs parallel with the road. Focal point is where the church and pub are sited. The imposing Punch Bowl dates from 1638, alongside is Holy Trinity church. A quoits pitch is on the green below the pub, while Hazel Brow Farm is a visitor attraction with a café. From the pub head west on the grassy roadside bank past the church to a minor junction. Just beyond this you join the road briefly just as far as the Wesleyan church of 1901 and adjacent Literary Institute and Assembly Room of 1909. Behind is a large, sloping burial ground.

Access roads and grass ways on the right now keep you off tarmac, running a parallel course past several dwellings. At the end house its access road slants away, but as it doubles sharply back down to the road, take a firm track straight ahead above a wooded bank. After a ford/footbridge it emerges to climb away: follow it only briefly past some scrub, then bear left across sloping pasture. Above a moist spring advance to briefly join the wall below. Before the end a path slants left down into trees, dropping to a gate onto the road. Short-cut the Crackpot junction by crossing the grassy triangle down onto the side road dropping to Isles Bridge.

Don't cross but take a path on the left to follow the Swale downstream, clinging to its bank for a good mile and a half. This section of riverbank, even by Swaledale standards, is sheer pleasure. An intriguing early section involves the flat top of a wall after which a wooded bend sees normal progress. Much further on the path enters Feetham Wood, and soon a guidepost indicates the end of the riverbank walk. Though a thin path continues, the true path is sent left and up the wooded bank onto the road.

Turn right for a few minutes to pass a solitary house. Immediately after take a stile on the left, and ascend past it to a gateway behind. Now climb the very steep field to a gate at the top right corner. A pause will be welcome to look back over the valley to Harkerside Moor. Ahead is a surprisingly populated scene. Cross to a stile and then to the house ahead, using a stile to its left. Ascend near the wall to a stile half way up, and cross the base of a field to another with a gate/stile behind. Just above is another stile alongside a cottage at Brockma Gill. From a stile on the left cross a field bottom to a gate at the end above the next house. Go right to merge into its drive, which leads out as a rough road to a gate onto grassy moorland.

Simply remain on this, passing another house and rising to a brow. The track continues across the moor past Gallows Top onto an open road on Feetham Pasture. Cross straight over along an access track serving two cottages. A thin path continues on, quickly reaching a corner of the moor where it becomes enclosed. Becoming more tightly enclosed it drops pleasantly down to emerge onto the hairpin bend of an access road. Turn left to drop back into Low Row.

The Punch Bowl Inn, Low Row

*3¹4 miles
from Healaugh*

**A memorable ascent of
Swaledale's best known and
shapeliest heathery hill**

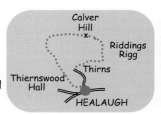

*Start Village centre (GR: 017990), parking area at east end
Map OS Explorer OL30, Yorkshire Dales North/Central
Access Open Access, see page 5*

       Healaugh was once the important manor herebouts, but today is merely a sleepy backwater of tidy stone cottages. Turn up the side road past a trio of stone troughs, and at an open green at the top bear left on a short access road: keep left as it runs on by a bungalow. Immediately after turn right on an enclosed grassy path. At the end a corner stile puts you into a field. Cross the field top to another at the end, then bear right through one and away with the wall on your left to a stile onto an enclosed driveway. Turn up this to approach Thiernswood Hall.

       The track keeps left of the house to enter trees, becoming a path: at the end ignore a stile in front and take a gate on the right into lovely open country. Rise to find a stile in the wall corner just above, from where a delightful green carpet rises through bracken. It spirals up in company with the left-hand wall, into more open moorland to meet a rough access road at the house at Nova Scotia. Advance on the continuing improved grassy track beyond the house, soon rising grandly through heather beneath a walled enclosure to merge with another track just beyond. Wooded Barney Beck is below you. Just yards to the left bear right up a thinner, broad way to the corner of another walled enclosure.

       This is the turning point: making use of Open Access, a thin trod ascends past reeds outside the enclosure. At the top corner a grassy way points up the slope above, through sparse heather to quickly gain a low nick on the skyline. Expansive moorland views are joined by the sudden appearance of Arkengarthdale ahead. Follow a pleasant path right, raking up the flank to pass beneath a cairn and a rash of stones, with Calver Hill's highest reaches just ahead. Remain on the path which runs a delightful course across a level plateau where the heather now peters out. Remain on this path traversing beneath the higher ground left, on through a further heather patch before slanting left up to a small cairn on the skyline. The substantial summit cairn is a couple of minutes further.

       The summit of Calver Hill is a classic Swaledale viewpoint, with much of the valley on show. More distant features are the A66 crossing Stainmore, and the North York Moors skyline. Leave by dropping right, your goal being a solitary section of sturdy wall on Riddings Rigg, at the foot of the immediate steeper slopes. A faint path slants right down by a scattering of stones, improving as it curves down to follow the wall down to its far end. Here turn right, within yards a clear path forming in the heather. This drops pleasantly down to a hard access track at a wall corner. Turn right, soon descending with bird's-eye views of Healaugh. It slants down to a solitary house and then down to Thirns Farm. Here turn left, at once becoming surfaced to drop steeply back into the village.

Calver Hill from the descent path

*3³4 miles
from Langthwaite*

**A valley walk yet with
splendid views of
this relatively
little-known dale**

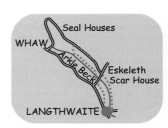

Start Village centre (GR: 005024), car park on road above
Map OS Explorer OL30, Yorkshire Dales North/Central

      Langthwaite is capital of Arkengarthdale, the Swale's
major side-valley. This tiny village comprises two distinct sections.
Along the 'main' road are strewn a miscellany of buildings, while
the other half stands below the road on the east bank of Arkle
Beck. In amongst is the Red Lion, one of Arkengarthdale's two
pubs, a cosy place which has the appearance of a bookshop as much
as an alehouse. The other pub, the CB (after local landowner
Charles Bathurst) stands on the road beyond the church.
Langthwaite was the centre of the dale's lead mining industry.
      Cross the bridge into the centre and leave by a rough
lane on the left before the road climbs away. From a gate at the
end a path crosses the field, through a gateway to a stile at the
end. The way continues across two more fields to a house, with Scar
House shooting lodge behind. Follow its drive down to Scar House's
wider drive, and head up it only a few strides to locate a path
through the trees. Over a small footbridge it quickly emerges into
a field. The thin path drops down nearer Arkle Beck, past a tiny
barn to a stile into a large beckside pasture. This is crossed parallel
with the beck to a stile onto the Stang road at Stang Bridge.
      Cross over for an appreciable pull up the road opposite:
this quiet byway is followed for a considerable time. Early on you
pass the former Eskeleth chapel. Opening out in grassy pasture it
runs on to a gate at High Eskeleth to level out on bracken-clad Low
Moor. The road is sufficiently elevated to give good views across

the remote upper dale to the old workings of Whaw Moor and Great Punchard Gill. Just before the end of the moor a couple of seats occupy a grassy knoll. Here a slim path doubles back left down through bracken, swinging right to a gate at the bottom. Entering a pasture slant right down the wallside, doubling back down to the isolated house of Greenbank. Pass left of it, and through a gateway a grassy way slants down to join a path by Arkle Beck. Turn left on this, enjoying some attractive wooded moments. Ignoring a foot-bridge on the beck continue through open pasture, still enjoying the tree-lined beck to emerge by a house. Just beyond, a footbridge is reached just one field short of Eskeleth Bridge's graceful arch. Cross the footbridge and turn downstream to a stile on the road. Before taking the right-hand of two gates opposite, a short detour up the road reveals a hexagonal powder house surviving from lead mining days sat in a field just over the wall on the right.

Back at the gate a drive heads away past a house, with the church ahead, and Scar House up to the left. Becoming enclosed it swings left towards Old School House: just before it take a stile on the right and a path crosses to join the Scar House drive. Follow this right to emerge onto the road by St Mary's church. Turn left on the footway to return through the rest of Langthwaite. En route you pass a Wesleyan Chapel of 1882, WCs, and a former Wesleyan Sunday School of 1923. *Arkle Beck at Eskeleth*

*4 miles
from Langthwaite*

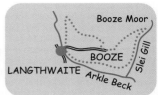

**A fine combination of beck
and moorland surrounds
in the colourful heart
of Arkengarthdale**

*Start Village centre, (GR: 005024), car park on road above
Map OS Explorer OL30, Yorkshire Dales North/Central*

For a note on Langthwaite see page 32. Cross the bridge into the heart of the village and turn right behind the first house. A broad track traces Arkle Beck downstream before striking away into a wood. At a fork keep left, rising out of the trees at a gate to cross a field to another gate. Fell End rises ahead with Fremington Edge stretching beyond. While the main track drops to Storthwaite Hall, your way is the grassy path straight ahead. Ignoring an early fork left it crosses several enclosures alongside Slei Gill until a stile heralds arrival at the old lead workings. A superb, embanked green track winds straight on between spoil-heaps. Slei Gill was the scene of much mining activity, but all is now peaceful. Looking back, Calver Hill rises across the main valley.

A steady, delectable grassy rise leads to an old gateway, and the confines become narrower. At this point leave by another inviting green way doubling sharply back left immediately before the gateway. It runs a very gentle slant looking down on the mining site, through an old wall to a solitary barn. Past this it runs through further mining remains, past an arched level and rises gently to a wall corner. Here a farm track leads along the wallside above the site to a corner gate behind a barn. Leaving the moor, it runs on a field top to a gate where it becomes briefly enclosed to reach Town Farm at Booze. Booze is a jovially named little settlement perched on a green patchwork hillside, its only link with the outside world being the lane from Langthwaite. At the other end follow the concrete access road up through the hamlet.

Levelling out to leave the houses, it runs on with a parallel drive above. After this joins, continue a little further until another drive (Fountain Farm) doubles sharply back uphill at a grassy triangle. Go a short way up it to a ruin before reaching the grounds, then slant back left up an inviting path, becoming sunken to rise between old walls to a bridle-gate to the top. As it swings right towards a gate take a thin way straight ahead, but leave this too in favour of a thin trod tracing the sturdy wall on your right. This clings tightly by the wall as it heads away to Booze Common, curving round high above the main valley. This colourful terrain soon reveals Langthwaite below.

On through modest mining remains, a gateway in an old wall corner admits to more open country. The trod slants gently right to a wall-gap, contours round to a stile, then on to a crumbling wall corner at the end. You are now looking directly down on the church. The trod resumes with a fence on your left to a stile at the end. A faint way contours above the steep wooded bank demanding caution, maintaining a generally level course below a craggy wall and past scattered rocks. At the end is another stile into a field. While the fence drops steeply away, slant more gently down to a corner, then drop left onto a thin bridle-path. Double back left on this through a bridle-gate into trees, and a super path runs a gentle slant down the wood. It continues for some time before joining the steep Booze road just above the roofs of Langthwaite.

Arkengarthdale from Booze Common

*4 miles
from Reeth*

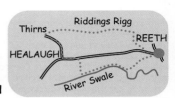

**A lovely village reached
by riverbank, returning
on the edge of moorland**

Start Village centre (GR: 038992), roadside parking
Map OS Explorer OL30, Yorkshire Dales North/Central

Reeth is capital of Swaledale within the National Park. It boasts an enviable position on the slopes of Calver Hill, well above the Swale and Arkle Beck. Central is a large, sloping green, with the main buildings stood back on all sides. This old market town exudes a confident air, with hoary inns, shops, tearooms and Post office alongside the green: there is also a National Park Centre and craft centre. Unfortunately parking limitations result in an untidy scene around the green in summer, amplified when market traders set up stall on Fridays. Indelibly linked with lead mining days, Reeth was once much more populous. There is an absorbing folk museum, while annual agricultural shows and festivals add cultural attractions.

From the green pass along the front of the Kings Arms and Black Bull to a contrastingly tiny green at Anvil Square. Across it, to the right, a sign 'to the river' sends a snicket off between walls. It emerges onto a narrow road: go left to join a suburban street. Turn left to a T-junction, then right along the narrow lane to its demise at the last house. This continues as a rough lane: Harkerside Moor dominates across the Swale. At the end turn left down a narrow, leafy footway to emerge overlooking the river. The path bears right through two fields to a suspension footbridge.

Don't cross but turn upstream, a good path clinging to the bank to emerge into open pasture. A delectable section follows on grassy banks: becoming part-enclosed again the path runs to adjacent stiles at stepping-stones on the Swale. Leave the river here by following the wall away to a gate up onto the valley road at the entrance to Healaugh. Go left into this sleepy backwater of stone cottages. Turn up the side road past a trio of stone troughs, and passing a green at the top the road climbs out of the village through a gate. It continues more steeply up colourful slopes to end at the farm buildings of Thirns. As it forks into access tracks, take the right-hand one climbing steeply to a cottage before continuing up to find level ground. Calver Hill is immediately above as the track runs across the moor, now with a wall for company. When it finally turns in to a gate, a more inviting track continues on, soon rejoined by the wall to cross pleasantly along the moor edge.

Above the farm of Riddings the track drops gently down, with the full length of Fremington Edge ahead. As it becomes firmer and bends left, keep straight on the more inviting grassy path ahead to a prominent cairn just short of the next wall-corner: here take a final look back to the shapely crest of Calver Hill. Just beyond is a recess and a gate where the green way of Skelgate waits to deliver you into Reeth. Its enchanting start is overtaken by exuberant undergrowth, and as the walls are replaced by foliage it becomes stonier underfoot. Just past a bend where a farm track crosses, leave at a stile by a gate on the right. Slant left down through a gateway and down to a stile in the bottom corner behind the village school. Just below it a bridle-gate puts you into a short snicket onto the valley road alongside the school on the edge of Reeth. Go left on the footway back down into the centre.

Market at Reeth

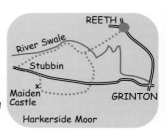

REETH

River Swale

Stubbin

Maiden ˣ Castle

GRINTON

Harkerside Moor

4½ miles
from Reeth

A beautiful, richly varied walk by riverbank and moorland, with outstanding views and a historic gem

Start Village centre (GR: 038992), roadside parking
Map OS Explorer OL30, Yorkshire Dales North/Central

For a note on Reeth see page 36. From the green pass along the front of the Kings Arms and Black Bull to a contrastingly tiny green at Anvil Square. Across it, to the right, a sign 'to the river' sends a snicket off between walls. It emerges onto a narrow road: go left to join a suburban street. Turn left to a T-junction, then right along the narrow lane to its demise at the last house. This continues as a rough lane. Looking over the river, Harkerside Moor dominates the dale. At the end turn left down an enclosed leafy footway to emerge overlooking the Swale. The path bears right through two fields to cross a suspension footbridge.

Head away from the bridge to the foot of the bank, crossing a simple wooden bridge to turn right on a grass track past a section of wall. At the wall-end take a gate in the fence on the right and the path meanders back to the river. Forge on in glorious surroundings to reach stepping-stones opposite Healaugh. Advance a little further to a bridle-gate, then the path slants left up the steep bank to a wall above. Your lush green way now runs a level course high above the river, with outstanding views to Healaugh backed by Calver Hill. Remain with the wall until passing through a gate/stile in an intervening fence. Here your path rises left to a gate, just above which a green way rises to an unfenced moor road.

Double back up the road as far as the second bridleway branching right, just as the wall below returns. Don't follow it, but trace an initially thinner path rising slightly left up the moor. This quickly becomes a fine green path climbing to a skyline tree. Arrival here is a splendid moment, for Maiden Castle is literally beneath your feet. This ancient earthwork is a defensive site of the Iron Age Brigante tribe: a deep ditch surrounds a tall bank, and the whole is largely unbroken other than its gateway at the far side.

The path largely fades here: cross to the far side of the earthwork, then continue on across virgin heather. This rougher section is short-lived, as sheeptrods ease progress across to a barn at a wall corner. Here a path slants right, soon forking; take the fading upper one to rise through heather to meet a very distinct path along the edge of a modest plateau. High above is the stony scarp of Harkerside Moor. Turn left, enjoying a grand stride as it angles gently down the moor. Broadening, it drops across to a corner gate where fence and wall meet. Joining a firmer track, pass through the gate and follow its green course down the wallside to a gate onto a road below. There is a good view of Reeth above the lazily winding river, backed by the long skyline of Fremington Edge.

Cross to a gate left of Bleak House and bear right down a steep field to a gate in front of a ruinous farm. Now bear right to a stile part way down, then down to a small gate below, left of a cottage. From another just behind it descend a big pasture to the far left corner, where a stile puts you onto a bridleway by the river flats. Go left to the suspension bridge and retrace opening steps.

Maiden Castle, looking to Calver Hill

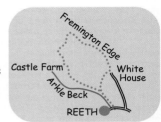

*4½ miles
from Reeth*

**A dramatic moorland edge
with extensive views of
Arkengarthdale precedes
a beckside return**

*Start Village centre (GR: 038992), roadside parking
Map OS Explorer OL30, Yorkshire Dales North/Central
Access Open Access, see page 5*

For a note on Reeth see page 36. Descend the green and
follow the Richmond road to Reeth Bridge on Arkle Beck. After
crossing, take a stile on the left and follow a wallside track left:
Fremington Edge dominates high above. When the track leaves go
straight ahead to a gate at the end. Cross to the right of a barn
ahead and along to a stile at the end. Now bear right to follow a
wall along to a stile in it above a wooded bank. Leaving the valley
floor, cross to a stile opposite then rise on a faint way past a barn
to a gate/stile above. Here is a crossroads of ways to which you will
return. Now on the steep base of Fremington Edge, take the thin
path rising away, bearing slightly left to ascend close by an old wall.
This pleasant way meanders steeply up, part-hollowed, to a brief
level halt. Views look back up-dale to Harkerside beyond Calver Hill.

Here take a right fork, slanting up a groove then gently
up to a top right corner stile by the isolated White House. A grassy
way rises left up a bracken bank to join a stony close road: turn left,
passing through a gate. Scattered about are old chert quarries:
chert was a flint used in pottery. A little more climbing gains the
crest of Fremington Edge. The track swings sharp right at a guidepost where you instead make use of Open Access and opt for an
inviting path left through moor grass. This magnificent stride along
the edge remains your course for some time. Relieved of that steep

40

ascent, savour dramatic views: across the valley is Calver Hill, with tree-lined Arkle Beck far below. The path varies but remains clear throughout. It rises very gently to a substantial cairn amid mining remains, then along to the end of a sturdy wall on the edge. A stile sends you along, all the way to pass through two crumbled walls.

Approaching the second crumbled wall is a cairn just in front: yards before this is your point of departure, as a thin path doubles back left. It slants down between rashes of stones to a hollow at the base of the upper edge, then doubles back right on a grassy shelf back towards the old wall. With Castle Farm House directly below, the path drops again, slanting left down a groove towards the intake wall. Just short of it veer left to join and follow it left. Through an old gateway the path continues down above the wall, becoming clearer to pass higher above it as a fence takes over: the path runs on down to a gate in a wall ahead. Entering scattered woodland it runs on to merge with a path at an old gateway just above Arkle Beck. Passing through the gateway the broad path forks left, ignoring one dropping to the beck. After a short amble through trees you emerge through a gateway amid colourful country. The broad path forges on alongside a fading wall on the right. After the second of two further gateways you curve round to the cross-paths on the outward route: pass through the stile on your right and drop down past the barn to return the way you came.

Calver Hill from Fremington Edge

*4¹2 miles
from Grinton*

**Easy walking with valley
scenery and distant
views on the return**

*Start Village centre (GR: 046984), roadside parking
Map OS Explorer OL30, Yorkshire Dales North/Central*

Grinton is the only settlement of any size on the south
bank of the Swale. At the centre are the Bridge Inn, St Andrew's
church, a former Literary Institute of 1903, and WCs. Until a chapel
was established at Muker in 1580, Grinton parish was one of the
largest in the land, extending the full length of the dale to the
Westmorland border. From the pub cross the bridge and turn right
on a path enjoying a good spell downstream on the Swale's wooded
bank until emerging into open pasture. Just ahead, a wooded bank
forces the path up to a stile onto Marrick Priory's access road.
Double back briefly left to a stile on the right to commence a
largely faint route through the fields. Head away, rising gently to
find a gate/stile up to the left of a fence corner. Good views look
back up-dale to Harkerside Moor and Calver Hill. A string of stiles
of various design lead you through the fields, aiming for the priory
tower. A nice wooded bank rises to the left, while Ellerton Moor
fills the skyline ahead. In the last field slant down to a corner gate
back onto the road at the farm entrance.

The priory was founded in its pastoral riverside setting
early in the 12th century for Benedictine nuns, and the greater
part of the remains have been converted into a residential youth
activity centre. Access is restricted to a gaze round the exterior:
alongside is Abbey Farm. After a cattle-grid by the buildings, take
a gate on the left where a green path rises to a bridle-gate into
Steps Wood. A gem of a flagged path climbs through it, the Nuns'
Causey still serving its original purpose of linking priory with village.

Leaving the wood a grassy path remains with the right-hand wall as the going finally eases, and through a gate by a barn it continues as a grassy track to enter Marrick. The old Wesleyan Chapel of 1878 stands on the left, with the former St Andrew's church of 1858 on your right. The village stands at a blustery thousand feet up, and though today a sleepy backwater, it knew far busier times in the heyday of lead mining.

At the first junction turn left up to the through road, and go left past a farm. Shortly after a dip beyond the brow, take a stile on the left and follow a wall away. At a stile cross to its other side and remain with it all the way. An early brow reveals Calver Hill, with Reeth soon appearing beneath it. Through two intervening gates/stiles the way runs to a gate onto the old Reeth-Richmond highway at Reels Head. A steep descent of this quiet lane ensues, noting a well-preserved limekiln on the right. Part way down, beyond a drive to The Hagg on the right, look out for a wall-stile on your left. From here slant right down the large pasture which is the one you crossed after the Marrick Priory lane. Bear right lower down it to rejoin your outward route at the stile onto the road, retracing steps along the riverbank to finish.

The Swale at Grinton

*4½ miles
from Marske*

**Splendid varied surroundings
in a little-known side valley,
featuring high quality
woodland and moorland**

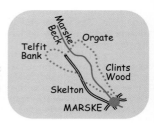

*Start Village centre (GR: 104004), parking by bridge
Map OS Explorer OL30, Yorkshire Dales North/Central
or Explorer 304, Darlington & Richmond
Access Open Access, see page 5*

Marske is a delightful place on, but largely outside, the National Park boundary. It differs immensely from other villages of the dale, with its cosy, mellow cottages sat amongst colourful gardens and embowered in noble trees. The large hall, once home of the Hutton family, survives as flats, and its exterior and grounds still impress. Above the centuries-old bridge is the still older church of St Edmund, with much Norman work.

Climb from the bridge to the road junction above the church, and take the road left. When it turns uphill advance on the level 'no through road': note the old sundial alongside. Last of the houses is a former school: here the road loses its surface as it opens into a field, with views over the valley and wooded banks to the right. Passing the scattered dwellings at Clints, a former chapel features. A broad carriageway forges on, giving a charming walk through the sylvan Clints Wood. Not far beyond the last dwelling the way starts a sustained rise through the trees to a fork: here bear left on a broad path where the main track continues rising. A gate is soon reached to emerge into open pastures beneath the limestone cliffs of Clints Scar. The superb green way runs on to approach Orgate Farm. Just before it turn down the access road to cross Marske Beck by footbridge or ford. Orgate Force is seen just upstream.

The access road climbs to a junction by a large barn, where turn right along Telfit's long farm drive, shadowing a wall all the way. This quickly passes through a gate into open country beneath the bracken flanks of Telfit Bank. Only a short way along, after a small barn and as far as a gate on the right where the first field ends, take a grass track slanting left into bracken. It quickly narrows to a path, becoming clear as it rises alongside its original sunken way. Soon turning sharply to slant left, a steady rise leaves the bracken and eases out on approaching a grassy track and wall at the top of the bank. Delightful views look over this charming side valley. Turn left on the green way, dropping quickly to a gate off the bank, where it becomes enclosed to drop down onto a back road.

Turn briefly right to locate a stile on the left after a small barn. Cross the field diagonally to a stile beneath a row of trees, then follow a fence away. When it turns left beyond an intervening bridle-gate go straight on to drop to the substantial stone-arched Pillimire Bridge. Just before it is the surprising sight of an old waterwheel stood in isolation. Across the bridge a path turns right, crossing the bank to meet the beck again. Here the higher option curves above a potentially muddy beckside section before curving down the bank to a bridle-gate into trees. The beckside path quickly reaches stone steps up onto Marske Bridge.

The Marske Valley from Telfit Bank

⟨20⟩ —————— HUDSWELL WOODS

3³⁄4 miles from Richmond

**Fine woodland and riverbank
on the edge of a classic town**

Start **Town centre
(GR: 171008), car parks**
Map **OS Explorer 304, Darlington & Richmond**

The gateway to Swaledale is a remarkable town dominated by its castle high above the Swale. The enormous 12th century keep watches over the whole town including, at its feet, the Market Place. Within its sloping cobbles is Holy Trinity church, incorporating shops and the Green Howards Museum. Lined by shops and pubs the Market Place is used as a bus station as well as for its original purpose on Saturdays: a market cross is still in evidence. Outside of the square from which narrow ways radiate are St Mary's church, Grey Friars Tower and the Georgian Theatre: dating from 1788 it has been restored to serve its original function. The military presence around the town is due to the proximity of Catterick Camp.

From the south-west corner of Market Place descend New Road, quickly forking left on a cobbled way that drops beneath an arch onto Bridge Street. Go left past The Green to cross the Swale on Green Bridge, looking back at a classic castle view. Immediately across take a broad path upstream: over the river is Culloden Tower. At an early fork keep left, a broad path slanting gently up through Billy Bank Wood, beneath a big quarried face and then a long line of smaller crags to a sharp corner looking down on a bend of the river. The path resumes at mid-height through the trees, before long slanting down to a gate into a riverside pasture. Cross to a path by the river and go left on a broad green way to reach (but not cross) a footbridge on the Swale accessing WCs at Round Howe car park.

Continue upstream through Hudswell Woods, an encounter with a sandy beach preceding the finest section in company with the river. Past an old quarry a fork is reached: again take the left one, slanting gently up to mid-height and passing beneath substantial cliffs. Further, at a fork ignore the right branch dropping to the river and keep on a little further to reach Hudswell Steps just short of the wood edge. This is the uphill bit, but at least you don't start at the bottom! Turn to ascend until meeting a cross-paths just short of the wood top. Go left, on through a gate/stile with a view down to Lownethwaite Bridge. From the fork behind keep left to remain on the wood top into Calfhall Wood, maintaining this until forced up a few steps into a field. Go left through a bridle-gate to another that puts you back in the trees. Resume as before, soon reaching a fork. This time take the stile out of the trees into open pasture.

Angle away to a bridle-gate in a hedge, then on with the hedge to a stile at the end. Cross an open area to a path junction: a stile sends a thin path on the wood top to escape at another stile. Go left again, outside the wood through several hedgerows before a short-lived section revisits the wood. On emerging curve round the wood edge a little further, but before the corner bear right to a stile in a hedge: the castle appears ahead. Maintain this slant to another stile, then cross between equine enclosures before slanting through two more stiles. Now bear right across a larger pasture to a dip where the wood comes in. A path forms to run to a stile back into the trees: ignore it and keep on the grass path above the wood to a kissing-gate at the corner where a firm path enters the trees. This runs along the top before slanting down a part sunken way to emerge onto the road on the other side of the house where you began.   *Richmond Castle*

21 — OLD GANG SMELT MILL

2 miles from Low Row

A bonus walk, because this lead mining landmark is too good to miss

Old Gang Smelt Mill
Old Gang Beck
Surrender Bridge
from Low Row

Start Surrender Bridge (GR: 988998), parking area at moorland road junction a mile to north
Map OS Explorer OL30, Yorkshire Dales North/Central

From the parking area descend to the bridge and as the road climbs away, take a firm track on the left. Running above Old Gang Beck it gains only a little height as it takes about a mile to reach the Old Gang Smelt Mill. This is the best known and most evocative of Swaledale's mining sites, dominated by a tall, intact chimney. On the hillside above are the remains of the former peat store. Either return the way you came, or for more interest advance past the main workings - and an old arched level on the right - to a stone-arched bridge on the left before the track starts climbing away. Cross and double back downstream on a thin, level path just above the beck. The going gets a little tight then opens out to run above slopes of spoil to a ruin opposite the main site, a splendid vantage point. A few yards further curve right, down off the end and down to re-cross the beck. Rejoin the track to return to Surrender Bridge.

At Old Gang Smelt Mill